imagine

A WORLD

by ROB GONSALVES

IMAGI

A New World

atheneum

Atheneum Books for Young Readers • New York London Toronto Sydney New Delhi

_A_
atheneum

ATHENEUM BOOKS FOR YOUNG READERS
An imprint of Simon & Schuster Children's Publishing Division
1230 Avenue of the Americas, New York, New York 10020
Copyright © 2015 by Rob Gonsalves
To learn more about Rob Gonsalves's work,
please visit robgonsalves.com
All rights reserved, including the right of reproduction
in whole or in part in any form.
ATHENEUM BOOKS FOR YOUNG READERS
is a registered trademark of Simon & Schuster, Inc.
Atheneum logo is a trademark of Simon & Schuster, Inc.
For information about special discounts for bulk purchases,
please contact Simon & Schuster Special Sales at
1-866-506-1949 or business@simonandschuster.com.

The Simon & Schuster Speakers Bureau can bring authors to
your live event. For more information or to book an event, contact
the Simon & Schuster Speakers Bureau at
1-866-248-3049 or visit our website at www.simonspeakers.com.
Jacket design by Vikki Sheatsley; interior design by Ann Bobco
The text for this book is set in Centaur MT Standard.
The illustrations for this book are rendered in acrylics.
Manufactured in China
0715 SCP
First Edition
10 9 8 7 6 5 4 3 2 1
CIP data for this book is available from the Library of Congress.
ISBN 978-1-4814-4973-1
ISBN 978-1-4814-4974-8 (eBook)

For Lise

imagine a world . . .

. . . where the beauty that has fallen

can find a way to fly.

imagine a world . . .

. . . where songs in the night

   awaken sleeping streets

   with a melody each home welcomes

   with unlocked doors

   and open hearts.

imagine a world . . .

. . . where the challenge of riding on

rough and rocky seas

is also a chance

to climb the highest peak.

imagine a world . . .

. . . where even the deep, dark places

are treasure rooms of marvels,

silent echoes

of towers in the sun.

imagine a world . . .

. . . where each word,

each thought,

each turn of a page in a book

is the beginning of a bigger idea.

imagine a world . . .

. . . where city lights float from their frames

like a flurry of falling stars

to brighten your way.

imagine a world . . .

. . . where scissors snipping

through the golden air

conjure mountains that move.

imagine a world . . .

. . . where patience, practice, and balanced steps

make you a master of walking on air.

imagine a world . . .

. . . where with the help of a guide

and the strength of your mind,

you can visit the vastness beyond.

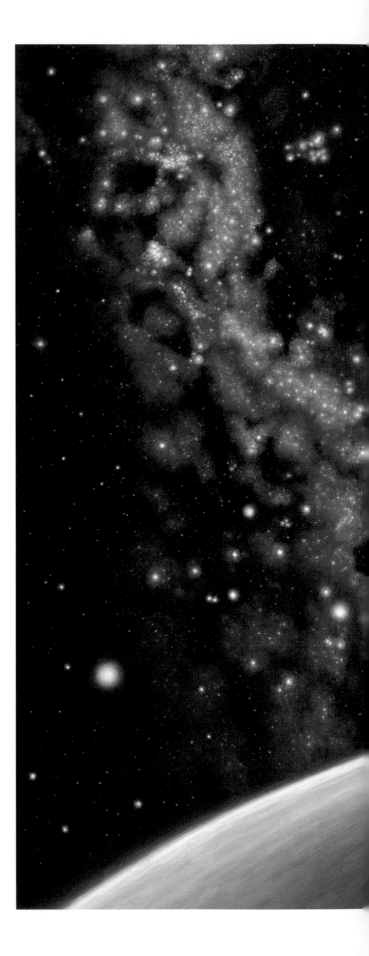

imagine a world . . .

. . . where the pull of the wind

is a hidden partner in a dance

that guides the performers to greatness.

imagine a world . . .

. . . where you're invited

to step out of your solitude

and join in the joy that you make.

imagine a world . . .

. . . where you can dive into a salty sky,

soar over submerged lands

into the secret garden of the sea.

imagine a world . . .

. . . where you can climb up to a valley,

paddle along a branch,

and feel the cool shade of a forest

from a single tree.

imagine a world . . .

. . . where the words you share with others

can bring them warmth and light.

imagine a world . . .

. . . where rushing water

steps and spins to life

in the rhythm of nature's dance.

imagine a world . . .

. . . where a breeze at the dawn of each new day

brings the scent of an adventure

that awakens the woods

and lets stones set sail.

imagine a world . . .

. . . where you can wander weightless on the Earth

and dream beyond the sky.

Imagine . . . this world.

This book was inspired by
the following paintings. . . .

Night Lights

Fall Color Flies

Performer

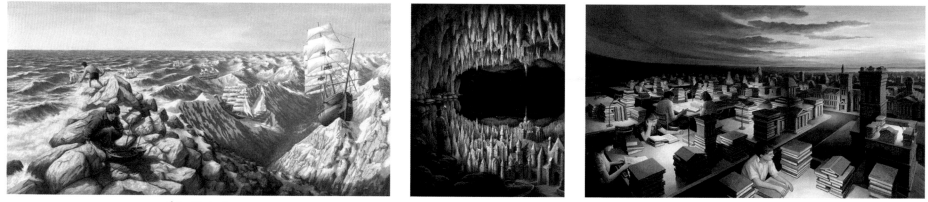

Alpine Navigation

As Above, So Below

Towers of Knowledge

Light Flurries

A Change of Scenery 2 (Making Mountains)

Aspiring Acrobats

Chalkboard Universe

Pulling Strings

Sweet City

Beyond the Reef

Waterlogged

The Space Between Words

Water Dancing

Sailing Islands

Phenomenon of Floating

To learn more about Rob Gonsalves's work, please visit robgonsalves.com